Nature's Children

CHIMPANZEES

Caroline Greenland

GROLIER

FACTS IN BRIEF

Classification of the Chimpanzee

Class: *Mammalia* (mammals)

Order: *Primates* (apes, monkeys, lemurs, people)

Family: *Pongidae* (people-like apes)

Genus: *Pan*

Species: *Pan troglodytes* (common chimpanzee)

Pan paniscus (pygmy chimpanzee)

World distribution. West and Central Africa.

Habitat. Varies with species.

Distinctive physical characteristics. Both species are tailless, and have a black coat. Their arms are longer than their legs. Common chimpanzee has pale skin. Pygmy chimpanzee has black skin, longer legs, a lighter build and a rounder head than the common chimpanzee.

Habits. Live in communities of 15 to 80. Use tools such as sticks and rocks. Build nests in trees each night to sleep in.

Diet. Fruit, vegetation, insects and occasionally animals.

Published originally as
"Getting to Know . . . Nature's Children."

This series is approved and recommended by the Federation of Ontario Naturalists.

This library reinforced edition is available exclusively from:

GROLIER

Old Sherman Turnpike, Danbury, Connecticut 06816

Contents

In the thickest part of the African jungle a loud hoot is heard. Birds fly away in fright. Excited screams are followed by more hooting and shrieking. Suddenly the trees are filled with chimpanzees swinging through the branches toward the noise. One chimp has found a tree filled with ripe fruit and it has called to all its friends. Soon they are feasting on the delicious fruit and chattering to each other.

As you can see, chimpanzees are very sociable —and they're also very intelligent. Turn·the page to learn more about these fascinating animals.

A Chimp Family

A mother chimp gently cradles her month-old baby in her arms. Her older youngster, now five years old, is fascinated with this new member of the family. As he reaches out to touch the furry little bundle, his mother pushes his hand away and turns her back on him.

It is hard for the youngster now that he is no longer the center of his mother's attention. She used to like to play with him. He shouldn't worry though. In a few months, his baby sister will be stronger and bigger. Then he will be able to teach her how to play tag and dangle from a tree with only one hand—and how to grab their mother's ear when she's looking the other way.

Even high up in a treetop, this baby chimp seems to feel perfectly safe and content in its mother's arms.

Big Apes, Little Apes

Chimpanzees belong to a group of animals called primates, which includes apes and monkeys. The larger apes are known as great apes. These include gorillas, orangutans and chimpanzees. The lesser apes, which are smaller, are gibbons and siamangs. Apes differ from monkeys in several ways. Apes do not have tails and they are bigger than monkeys. They also have larger brains and are considered to be more intelligent.

Many scientists believe that apes and human beings had a common ancestor long, long ago. Certainly apes have many similarities with people. They can stand upright, they have large brains and their bodies, muscles and blood types are similar to ours. And apes often behave exactly the same way we do.

In the wild, chimpanzees may live to be almost 40 years old.

Opposite page:
Pygmy chimp. The reason both the common and pygmy chimps stay on their own sides of the Zaire River is simple: chimpanzees cannot swim.

Land of the Chimpanzees

There are two kinds of chimps, the common chimpanzee and the pygmy, or bonobo, chimpanzee. The difference between them is not that one is much smaller than the other, as you might expect. Instead, the pygmy chimpanzee has longer legs, a lighter build and a more rounded head. It also has a black face, whereas the common chimp's is usually light.

The pygmy chimpanzee is found in rain forests in central Africa, between the Zaire and Kasai rivers. The common chimpanzee is found north of the Zaire River in west and central Africa.

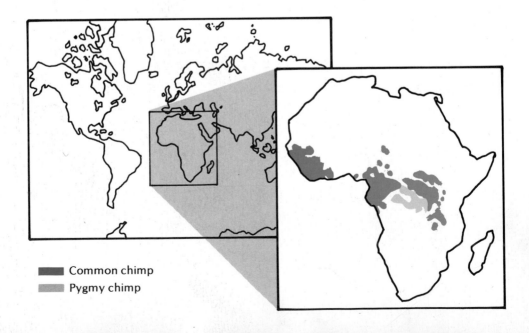

■ Common chimp
■ Pygmy chimp

*Male chimps may perform displays
even on sunny days to show others
how strong they are.*

Rain, Rain, Go Away

The area where chimpanzees live in Africa is near the equator. Temperatures there can vary from a very hot day (42°C or 108°F) to a cool night (10°C or 50°F). Throughout much of the chimpanzee's habitat there is a rainy season. From December to March it rains for long periods of time.

During rainstorms male chimps sometimes perform noisy displays, screaming and throwing things. Youngsters swing wildly through the trees as if they are trying to dodge the rain drops. Females may make nests and try to sleep through the storms. The only chimps that stay dry are the babies, snugly nestled between their mother's chest and arms.

Luckily chimps' thick coats help keep them warm even when they get wet. Once they are soaked, they often just sit in the open looking miserable. Intelligent as they are, they do not build shelters. However, when the rain finally stops they dry themselves off with leaves.

Hand

Foot

Weighing In

Chimpanzees are about the same size as a ten-year-old child. Most are about a metre (over 3 feet) tall with a few growing to 1.7 metres (5-1/2 feet). Adult males usually weigh 45 to 80 kilograms (99 to 176 pounds), though a large one may tip the scales at 90 kilograms (198 pounds). The females are shorter and lighter.

Although chimps look quite similar to humans, their arms are longer than their legs. They also have very long fingers but, just like you, they have opposable thumbs. This means that they can move their thumb around to meet their fingers, which allows them to pick up things easily. Chimps also have opposable big toes, so they can climb trees and grasp branches with their feet much more easily than you can.

The common chimp can be found in rain forests, woodlands and grasslands dotted with trees.

14

Swinging Through the Trees

Although chimpanzees can walk upright, they
only do so if they are angry, if their hands are
full or if they are trying to see over tall grass.
When chimps are on the ground they usually
"knuckle walk"—that is, they walk on all fours
but support the front part of their body on their
knuckles, not their palms.

Chimpanzees spend more than one-third of
their time in trees. Their extra long palms and
fingers give them a special hook grip that allows
them to swing easily from branch to branch.
Their opposable thumbs and big toes help to
make them fast and steady climbers.

"Now what do I do?"

Sensible Senses

Do you think you would be able to sneak up on a chimp? Not a chance. Chimps have large ears that stick out from the sides of their head. They can catch even the smallest sounds. They also have a keen sense of smell which helps them to find food and sniff out intruders. Their eyes face forward and they have the ability to perceive depth and color. This allows them to spot ripe fruit amidst the thick vegetation where they live. And with their excellent eyesight they notice everything that is going on around them.

Both male and female chimps may become bald as they grow older. You can tell this is a male chimp because its bald patch is triangular.

Chimp Communities

Chimpanzees live in communities of 15 to 80 members. Although they roam through a territory of up to 60 square kilometres (24 square miles), they spend most of their time each day in a small area under 4 square kilometres (1.5 square miles). The whole community is rarely seen together. Instead, smaller groups form for one or two days and then separate. New groups are constantly being formed. The only chimps who see each other daily are the family groups made up of a mother and her young offspring. Males may form temporary groups for patroling the borders of their territory and for socializing.

Although different chimpanzee communities may have overlapping ranges, it is difficult to know how they will react when they meet. Sometimes strangers are ignored and sometimes they are accepted. At other times they are attacked and driven away by groups of males.

*Chimps do not swim but they will
go into shallow water to cool off.*

Opposite page:
How do you think this chimpanzee is feeling?

Getting the Point Across

If you were pretending to be a chimp, how would you act? Most people would pant and hoot while jumping up and down. When a chimp behaves like this, it is excited or happy about something.

Chimpanzees seem to have many of the same emotions as humans—they can feel happy, sad, angry or frightened. They show their feelings in different ways, just as we do. They use sounds such as hoots, grunts and whimpers. Their faces can show all kinds of expressions including smiles and pouts. Body language is another way of letting others know how they feel. There is no mistaking a happy young chimp. It uses its *whole* body by twirling and somersaulting.

Chimpanzees are sociable animals. They greet old friends with hugs and kisses. They also like to hold hands and pat each other on the back. A frightened chimp may reach out to touch a member of its community to reassure itself. And if a chimp feels threatened it stands upright and bristles its hair to make itself look bigger.

Loud, Louder, Loudest

Imagine a fierce thunderstorm passing over an African forest. Rain is pelting down and lightning is flashing across the sky. The tree branches sway with the wind. Suddenly a male chimpanzee charges down a hill, swinging his arms wildly and screaming. He rips a bough from the nearest tree and beats the ground as he bounds through the wet grass. Then, up a tree he leaps, only to come crashing down with more loud hoots. Is he crazy? No, he is behaving the way many male chimps do in a thunderstorm. He is performing what is called a display.

Why a male chimp may display when there is a storm is something of a mystery, but on other occasions the reason for this noisy performance is more obvious. He is showing other males how strong he is.

You will hardly ever see a chimp relaxing in the sun—it prefers the shade.

What's for Lunch?

Over half a chimp's waking hours are spent eating, and much of the rest of its time is spent looking for food. Most of what a chimp likes to eat grows on trees. Fruit, leaves, seeds and bark all taste good to a chimp.

Fruit is one of the chimpanzee's favorite things to eat. Within their territory chimps know the exact location of all the different fruit trees. They even remember from one season to the next when the fruit will ripen.

When ripe figs are found, a chimp is not selfish. It barks, pants and hoots to announce the good news to other chimps in the community. Soon it will be joined by more chimps who grin and pat each other on the back before settling down to eat.

As well as vegetation, chimps also eat bird eggs, insects and honey. Once in a while they eat birds, antelopes, bush pigs and even monkeys although they have no organized system of hunting.

Tasty twigs.

Fishing for Termites

Chimpanzees are considered to be one of the most intelligent animals. They are able to solve problems by using their brains. And like people they have developed the ability to use tools.

Now a chimp likes a tasty meal of termites, but it's not easy to get at termites when they are inside their rock-hard mound. So a chimp finds a small twig or a thick blade of grass and trims it until it's just the right size to use as a "fishing rod." Then the chimp pokes the rod into a hole in the mound. The termites bite it and the chimp pulls it out and removes the insects with its lips. Delicious!

A young pygmy chimp plucks insects off blades of grass for a quick snack.

Tool Box

Catching termites is not the only thing chimps use tools for. They use sticks and rocks to break the hard outer coverings of some types of fruit. And when there isn't much water around, chimpanzees will make "sponges" to soak up water. First they chew up a mouthful of leaves. Then they roll the leaves into a ball and place it in a damp hole in a tree or wherever else hard-to-reach water is found. Finally they squeeze the sponge to have a cool drink.

Chimps sometimes use rocks and branches as weapons against other animals.

A refreshing drink on a hot day.

Looking Good

You use a comb or brush to keep your hair tidy. Chimps use their fingers and lips to groom themselves and each other. Two chimps sit close together. One parts the other chimp's hair and looks for old bits of skin and salt which it removes with nimble fingers or lips. Sometimes more than two chimps are involved in the grooming. It may surprise you to know that chimps do not have fleas. They do have the occasional tick or louse, however. These make crunchy treats!

Keeping neat and clean is not the main reason for grooming. More often than not a chimp is groomed when it is excited or worried. Grooming feels good and it helps calm down an upset chimp. Also, grooming helps the members of a community to feel close to one another. This sociable activity may go on for hours and may include as many as ten chimpanzees.

Adult chimps usually spend an hour
or so a day grooming.

Opposite page:
*A cool,
comfortable spot
to rest.*

Night Nests

How would you like to make your bed every day—from scratch? Chimps do. In fact, sometimes they even make two beds a day. One is for sleeping in at night and the other is for their afternoon nap.

How do they do it? First they select a strong base. A fork in a tree or two branches close together will do. This may be 10 metres (33 feet) above the ground—about as high up as the top of a telephone pole. Next the chimp forms a mattress by bending branches to cover the base. Each branch is held in place by one of the chimp's feet until the next branch is bent. Small twigs and leaves are then stuffed into the mattress to make it soft. Now for the test. The chimp lies down to see if it is comfortable. If the bed is not to its liking, more leaves are plucked and placed in the hard spots.

The only time a bed is shared is when a mother has a youngster under four years old. Young chimps are capable of making their own nests long before this but they seem to enjoy the companionship of their mother at night.

Mating

Chimpanzees can mate at any time of the year. Females are able to give birth after the age of six. At mating time, females are given special treatment in their community. They are groomed more often and food is shared with them. The females can relax and enjoy this unusual situation.

A female may sometimes mate with many males in her community. At other times the strongest male will chase away all the other males. Then he and the female go off alone together for days or even weeks. The baby is born eight months later. Chimps rarely give birth to twins.

A mother chimp is fiercely protective of her baby.

Bouncing Baby

A baby chimp is smaller than a human baby. It usually weighs less than 2 kilograms (4.4 pounds) and has a white tuft on its rump which fades as it grows older.

At first the little chimp is almost as helpless as a human baby. It cannot hold its head up or grasp its mother's hair. The mother chimp uses one arm to cradle her youngster close to her breast. This means she only has one free arm to use as she moves along the ground or through the trees. She must also stop often to nurse the little one. Its mother's milk will be its most important food for the next three or four years.

The other chimps in the community are curious and crowd around to take a peek. But not until the baby is a few months old will the mother allow them to touch it.

It's not long before a baby chimp begins to take an interest in its surroundings.

Playful Chimps

At about six months old, it is time for the youngster to start riding piggy back. Its mother gives it a boost onto her back and starts to walk slowly. At first the little one slips under her tummy in the old familiar riding position. But it must learn, so she pushes it back on top. After many tries and several weeks the youngster can hold on no matter how fast the mother moves.

Baby chimps spend a lot of time playing as they grow older. They love being tickled by their mother. They also enjoy pulling on her ears and wrestling. All these activities help the chimp to become more coordinated and agile.

After a hard day of playing it's nice to have a ride.

Growing Up

Soon the young chimp wants to explore the world beyond its mother's back. This means walking—on twos and fours!

You know how hard it is for a human baby to figure out how to crawl. Well, the same is true for chimps. They get their hands and feet all mixed up and spend a lot of time falling on their face. But by its first birthday, a chimp will be able to scamper along after the other youngsters in the community.

Now it's time for them to tackle trees. Wow—this is easy! After all, a chimp can dangle from a branch using one foot. You could do that too if your feet looked like your hands.

"Don't worry, I won't let you fall."

Lessons to Learn

A young chimpanzee learns by watching its mother. After it is one year old it helps her to build a nest to sleep in. It watches her fishing for termites and tries to do the same. After many attempts it is able to get a few termites. Soon the youngster's skills improve.

Young chimps do not leave their mothers until they are five to seven years old. It takes that long for them to learn everything they need to know. The females usually go on to new communities while the males stay in the community where they were born. And in a few years they are ready to have families of their own.

Words to Know

Bonobo Another name for the pygmy chimpanzee.

Display A noisy performance made by a male chimpanzee during a thunderstorm or to impress other males.

Groom To clean or brush, especially hair.

Knuckle walk When an animal, such as a chimpanzee or gorilla, walks on all fours but supports the front part of its body on its knuckles.

Mate To come together to produce young. Either member of an animal pair is also the other's mate.

Opposable thumb The kind of thumb that is separated from the fingers and can be moved around to meet them. Humans and a few animals, including chimpanzees, have opposable thumbs.

Primate An animal which belongs to the order *Primates*, such as a chimpanzee, monkey or human being.

Rain forest Lush tropical forest with heavy rainfall.

Territory Area that an animal or group of animals lives in and often defends from other animals of the same kind.

INDEX

Cover Photo: George Holton (Photo Researchers)

Photo Credits: Photo Researchers, pages 4, 7, 24; Walter Chandoha, page 8; Nancy Adams, pages 11, 27, 28, 39; Gerard Fritz (Canapress/Uniphoto Picture Agency), page 12; Stella Brewer (WWF-Photolibrary), pages 15, 16; Bill Ivy, page 19; Jay Foreman (Unicorn Stock Photos), page 20; Cincinnati Zoo, page 23; Stephen Krasemann (Peter Arnold/Hot Shots), page 31; Tom McHugh (Photo Researchers), pages 32, 43, 44; Philippe Oberle (WWF-Photolibrary), page 35; George Holton (Photo Researchers), pages 36-37, 40.